1. What

Understanding Stress

Do you ever feel that you are racing around but getting nowhere, unable to get to sleep at night because you are still worrying about how much you have left to do?

Do you wish you had more time for a social life or for relaxing? Do you find it hard to listen to what other people are saying, or get frustrated with the way others behave around you?

If so, you may be letting stress control your life - and may actually be risking your health as well as creating difficulties for those around you. This guide is designed to help you recognise and understand stress and to help YOU control it; stress will then work to your advantage.

Stress in itself is not harmful; in fact stress is essential for coping with life and for responding to sudden demands and challenges - such as changes at home or at work, achieving physical fitness, organising holidays, meeting deadlines, preparing for exams or interviews and so on.

For such situations you need this surge of adrenalin and, as a result, you will perform your task more effectively. However, when this level of stress continues over a longer period - for instance due to the pressures you are under or the way you respond to life around you - then you can actually be damaging your health: your body is only designed to cope with a short term 'stress response'.

Niggling headaches, aches and pains in joints, ulcers and appetite loss are all signs that you may be letting stress get the better of you, and you may not be able to get as much out of life as you could if you were relaxed.

Work your way through this guide, noting down your scores and action points in the personal spaces provided. When you have finished complete your own Personal Action Plan on pages 28 and 29.

Use the Stressdots on the card on the front cover to see how relaxed or stressed you are now, and learn how you can control your stress levels as you go through the guide. Start with the questions on the next page to assess how you are responding to life at the moment.

How stressed are you in your daily life?

Here are some questions which will reflect how stressed you are in your daily life - tick each one in the column which most clearly reflects how true this is for you, and then add up your scores at the bottom.

In the last few months how often have you:

	OFTEN	SOMETIMES	SELDOM	NEVER
Lost your appetite?				
Found you are constantly nibbling at snack food?				
Felt sick after eating?				
Bitten your nails or tapped your feet and fingers?				
Been restless?				
Found yourself getting angry or upset?				
Felt you have to work extra hard or late?				
Been worked up by heavy traffic or other travellers?				
Tried hard to win in sports?				
Tried hard to win in arguments?				
Struggled for perfection?				
Felt that you don't spend enough time with your family?				
Found it difficult to sleep at night?				
Used alcohol when under pressure?				
Used cigarettes to help when you are under pressure?				
Felt trapped by your lifestyle?				
Found you are too busy to do things you enjoy doing?				
Found it hard to make decisions?				
Worried about your future?				
Found it hard to concentrate?				
Suffered from headaches?				
Found yourself grumbling or moaning?				
Found it difficult to laugh or smile?				
Now add up the number of ticks in each column TOTAL TICKS				
Then multiply each column by	x3	x2	x1	x0
TOTAL				

Now add the four columns together: GRAND TOTAL

Check your result overleaf

Quiz Score

If you have more than 45 then your stress level is high. You may be a workaholic and you may be suffering from physical effects of stress. You definitely need to follow some course in stress management.

If you have between 35 and 44 then your stress level is still too high. There are some areas in your life you need to work on in order to enjoy life and be less stressed.

If you are in either of these first two categories you may feel too stressed to recognise what is happening or to take action; but take heart - the ideas and techniques set out in this guide are simple and fun to follow and you may notice an immediate improvement in your health and begin to enjoy life more.

If you have between 25 and 34 then your stress level is moderate but you could well do with a little more relaxation at times.

A score of below 25 indicates that you have got the balance about right! You show few signs of stress but do read on, it is worth learning how to relax so that you build your energy reserves for when you need them.

Write your quiz score in your personal space at the bottom of the page.

personal space

How stress affects you and your body

You have to only look around any group of people - whether in the doctor's waiting room, in a meeting at work, in a pub or just at home with the family - to see people in various states of tension.

Often there is high-pitched laughter, excitable, nervous chatter, a lot of bad language and tense arguing - all signs of stress! Although people may not realise it, all of the following are signs of stress.

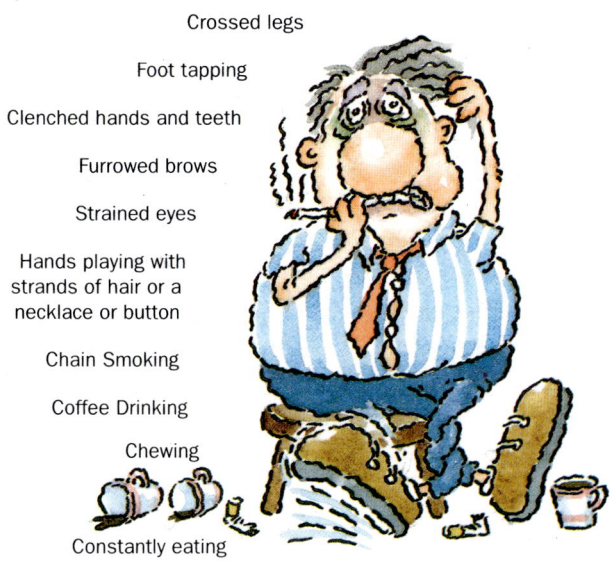

Crossed legs

Foot tapping

Clenched hands and teeth

Furrowed brows

Strained eyes

Hands playing with strands of hair or a necklace or button

Chain Smoking

Coffee Drinking

Chewing

Constantly eating

Write down in the personal space at the bottom of the page which stress signs you have noticed around you this week.

personal space

Effects of stress: short term

Short term stress is useful and gives you the impetus to act and respond to life's problems. When the stress system is on, many chemical changes occur in the body to prepare you to deal with exciting or challenging events. Learn to recognise them each time they happen. Learning to cope with stress begins with self-awareness.

When the action is over, your short term stress symptoms settle down to normal again and no harm will have been done.

In the short term the body adapts to normal stress and you remain balanced and healthy. If you notice any of these symptoms continuing when the stressful situation is over, you could actually be damaging your health.

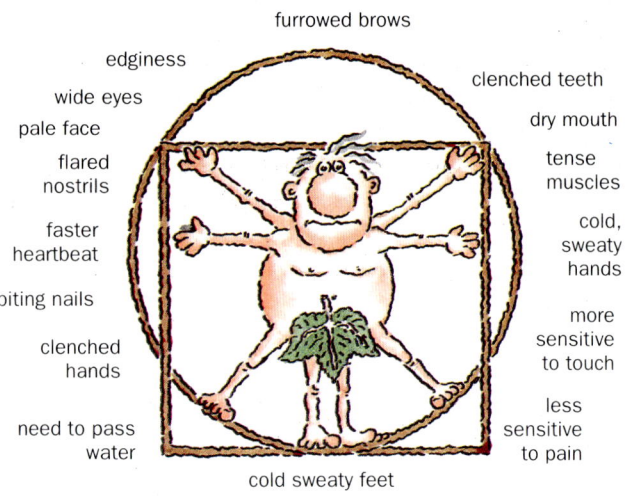

Have a look at this page and make a note of your short term stress symptoms in the personal space below.

personal space

The effects of stress: long term

Do you ever have difficulty sleeping at night? Or find it hard to concentrate during the day? Do you feel you are too busy to get anything done or to enjoy life? If so these may be signs that you are suffering from ongoing, 'long term' stress.

Why can't you sleep? It may be because you are living life at such a fast pace and are unable to switch off and slow down as you should towards bedtime. Your mind continues to work when you should be sleeping, and worrying about sleep then stops you from sleeping.

This type of long-term, prolonged stress is harmful to your body and can soon lead to a variety of other physical disorders:

• Appetite loss • Skin conditions • Headaches • Backaches • Ulcers and indigestion • Stomach problems • Neck and shoulder tension • Neck ache and leg ache • Chest tension • Constipation or diarrhoea • Heart problems • High blood pressure

Not to mention a variety of familiar emotional problems:

• Being on edge • Withdrawal • Feeling guilty
• Aggression • Depression
• Marital problems • Worry
• Blame • Fear
• Boredom • Insomnia
• Sexual problems
• Hyperactivity
• Excessive drinking
• Drug abuse

Have you suffered any of these stress-related problems recently, say in the last 12 months? If so, write any in your personal space below.

personal space

What makes you stressed?

Different people are affected by different stressors. Here are some examples of things that make people stressed. It is important that you recognise what makes you stressed, so mark below any of these which apply to you.

Tick if YES

Are you dissatisfied with your job?	
Are you dissatisfied with your home or social life?	
Do you have to spend a lot of time working, maybe also doing overtime to supplement your income?	
Does your lifestyle make you unhappy?	
Do you feel bored and trapped?	
Is time management a problem?	
Do you always have more than you can cope with in the day?	
Are you drinking too much coffee? (more than 3 cups a day)	
Do you find it difficult to motivate yourself?	
Do you drink more alcohol than you feel you need to?	
Do you eat many fatty or sugary foods?	
Are you missing out on fresh fruit and vegetables and salads?	
Do you feel unfit or overweight?	
Do you watch screens all day? (either computer or television)	
Do you have to perform tedious repetitive tasks all day?	
Are you 'negatively programmed-? (i e do you use words like 'It's terrible", "It's awful","I dread","I can't"?)	
Do you always have to struggle to make ends meet?	
Do you have to worry about debts and paying off loans/the mortgage?	
Do you spend a lot of time on the phone?	
Is your working environment uncomfortable, or poorly lit or ventilated, or very noisy?	
Do you fear for your promotional chances?	

continued. . .

	Tick if YES
Do you have to cope with constant changes at home or at work?	
Do you often feel there is conflict between home and work?	
Do you often argue with your work colleagues or family?	
Do you find it difficult to express yourself?	
Do you feel you are always being asked to do more than you can do?	

Now think of the six greatest causes of stress in your life - they may be listed above, or they may be different. It will help you to cope with them if you are aware of what they are, so write them down in your personal space now, so that you can refer to them later or discuss them with someone else. Next time anything stressful occurs, look at the colour of your Stressdot and see it turn black.

personal space

The effects of life's changes

Did you know that change itself causes you stress? The more change you have to cope with in one go, the more stressed you will feel. Stressful changes include not only the unpleasant experiences in life, but also happy events such as holidays, marriage and the birth of a child.

Life-events involve considerable changes and disruption, some of them more than others. In an ideal world the body can only handle one at a time. Look back over the last 6 to 12 months - mark the changes you have experienced.

- 100 • Death of someone close
- 73 • Divorce/separation
- 53 • Injury/illness
- 50 • Marriage
- 47 • Redundancy
- 45 • Retirement
- 39 • Birth of a child
- 38 • Change in finances
- 29 • Child leaving home
- 27 • Completing education
- 20 • Change at work
- 16 • Moving house
- 15 • Going on holiday
- 12 • Christmas
- 11 • Breaking the law.

Count up the total number of points for all your changes. If you have over 50 then it is very likely that these changes are making you feel stressed.

The body is not a machine. If circumstances become intolerable something will 'give', like a rubber band which is stretched too far, and you will make yourself ill. Give yourself time and space to adjust to the change in your life. Talk to somebody: remember a problem shared is a problem halved.

Understanding your personality

Your personality and behaviour will affect the way you react to situations in life. Certain behaviours will cause you to be more stressed when dealing with everyday events, and can even lead to stress disorders. No two people are alike and people will react differently, even within a family. Two main personality types have been identified - try this quiz to see where you stand. Tick any one which you think describes your behaviour.

In normal conversation I sometimes shout or stress certain words.	
I often speak faster or miss out words as I near the end of a sentence.	
I tend to feel guilty when I relax.	
I usually judge success by the ability to get a lot done quickly.	
I am usually in a hurry.	
I often get angry or tense when waiting in queues.	
I walk, talk and eat quickly.	
I often skim a page or miss things when reading.	
I often do more than one task at a time.	
I find it difficult to express my feelings.	
I get frustrated if people do things too slowly.	
I find it difficult to stick to speed limits and get impatient with other drivers.	
When on holiday I often miss lovely sights.	
I am constantly striving for material gain.	
If a conversation is about a subject that doesn't interest me, I pretend to listen while thinking about something else.	
I find fault with and criticise others.	
I am impatient with the speech of others (i.e. I finish their sentences or chase them with yes, yes, yes....)	
I grind my teeth.	
I am developing a nervous tic.	
I emphasise conversation with aggressive gestures (e.g. pounding the table with my fist).	
I am very competitive when I meet someone new.	
I get impatient at having to perform trivial tasks (like washing up).	
Now add up your total number of ticks TOTAL	

If you have ticked at least 10, you have more of what is called a 'type A' personality. If you have ticked less than 10 then you have more of a 'type B' personality. Now turn to the next page to see if you can recognise yourself.

Which personality are you?

A: 'The Hurrying Achiever'

You are likely to be a very hard worker and a perfectionist, seldom satisfied with your own and never satisfied with other people's performance, and always striving to do better.

You are seldom as effective as you would like to be, and are always short of time.

Your personality is likely to make you prone to high levels of stress.

Main characteristics

- Always in a hurry
- Impatient
- Does more than one thing at a time
- Tense and restless
- Poor listener
- Hates criticism
- Tendency to be aggressive
- Very competitive

Many of your stress problems may be caused by this type of personality - always rushing and doing everything at once. Remember, you don't have to rush to get things done.

'A' Traits   personal space

B: 'The Relaxed Listener'

You are generally observant of what goes on around you, and take life as it comes.

You are happy to work with and listen to other people, and are prepared to live with your own and other people's shortcomings.

You would make a patient teacher or cooperative student.

Your personality is likely to make you more resistant to high levels of stress.

Main characteristics

- Extremely laid back and easygoing
- Patient
- Calm and in control
- Co-operative with others
- Flexible
- Able to delegate and encourage others
- Takes breaks and rests when tired without feeling guilty
- Can take criticism

However there is no cut and dry dividing line - you may be a mixture of the two. Where do you think you are on the A-B line?

A _ _ _ _ _ _ _ _ _ _ _ _ _ _ _ _ _ _ B

Now make a note in your personal space of the key characteristics which you think describe your personality.

'B' Traits   personal space

Stress, fatigue and your health

Can you now recognise where you are on the following stress/burnout scale? Be aware of your own stressors and your limitations, and when you might be approaching burnout level.

Too little stress	**Optimum stress**	**Too much Stress**	**Burnout**
Boredom	Life is balanced	Constant feeling of having too much to do	Ill
Lethargy	Control		Depressed
Tiredness	Confidence	Aggressive	Exhausted
Worry about un-important things	Commitment	Always tired	
Can't be bothered	Happy	Tense	
Passive	Coping	Aches and pains	
Negative	Calm	Worry/anxiety	
	Assertive	Angry	
	Good relationship	Failing relationship	
		On edge	

Now you should have a better idea of how stressed you are and what is causing your stress - in terms of what changes are happening in your life, what your own personal stressors are, and how your personality makes you respond to stress. Now you can start to help yourself by learning how to control your stress and make it work to your advantage.

2. Act now to help yourself

Overcoming stress is something which you must learn to do: it doesn't just 'happen', but will come easily with practice. Read through the various lifestyle points and relaxation exercises which follow, and try out as many as you can to help you control your stress.

Relaxed breathing

It may sound obvious, but the WAY we breathe has a very dramatic effect on our well-being. Ensure that you change position every so often and try to get out in the fresh air for a short walk at lunch-time. Many people, and especially stressed people, adopt incorrect breathing habits without realising it, and these begin to feel normal. They need to be 'unlearned' and replaced with diaphragmatic breathing.

Try the following simple exercise:

• 1. Sit, or lie down on your back, and become aware of your breathing, its rhythm and depth (or shallowness), its speed.

• 2. Check whether you are comfortable and loosen any tight clothing around your waist and abdomen.

• 3. Put one hand on the upper part of your chest and the other on your abdomen just below your ribs.

IN...

- 4. First let your breath sigh OUT slowly.

- 5. Then breathe IN very gently feeling your abdomen rise a little under your lower hand.

- 6. Let your breath out again feeling your abdomen drop back and allow the outbreath to be a little longer than the inbreath.

- 7. Then pause for a moment and breathe in again. Only your lower hand should move as your correct abdominal or diaphragmatic breathing causes your abdomen to rise and fall rhythmically.

You should find that there is very little movement, if any at all, of your upper chest so your upper hand will remain still.

If you find this difficult or know that you have a tendency to hyperventilate, try another exercise:

Lie on your stomach, head resting on your hands, feet slightly apart, then relax and breathe deeply for a few minutes.

Practise abdominal breathing for 5 minutes every day along with the relaxation described on the next page and you will alleviate •feelings of tension and anxiety •dizziness •pins and needles •muscle cramps and chest pains, and you will soon notice the beneficial effects.

...OUT

Simple relaxation exercises

Relaxation is the body's natural antidote to stress. It is switching off and completely letting go - physically and mentally, and should be practised every day by everyone, not only people who feel stressed.

Try this simple exercise when you feel under pressure, it need only take 5 to 10 minutes:

- 1. Have a good stretch. Let go and let your breath sigh out gently as your shoulders drop to a comfortable relaxed position. You may need to pull your shoulders down and then allow them to settle comfortably. Moving your body gently, shrugging and wriggling or shaking, all help to prepare your muscles to let go, so don't be afraid to have a good wriggle or shake every now and again as well as a stretch.

- 2. Sit on a chair or lie on the floor and make yourself comfortable and, once you have become aware of your breathing, practise your abdominal breathing straight away.

- 3. Relax your jaw and your face - allow the expression to come off it for the time being - be passive.

- 4. Now try to let any tension go in your feet, ankles, calves, knees, thighs, abdomen, chest and arms and particularly in your neck.

You will find it much easier if your head is supported. Gently close your eyes.

- 5. Feel as if the chair, or the floor, is supporting your whole weight and that it is safe to let go.

- 6. Imagine a pleasant place and feel as if you are really there and rest a while.

Emphasise your type B 'Relaxed Listener' personality traits. Sometimes it doesn't hurt just to sit back and examine what may be causing your stress. You are 100% responsible for your own life and health.

Control your anger - say to yourself 'Anger is my enemy' - and calm down. Your work and home life will start to flourish when you become more relaxed.

The following exercise is for use in emergencies, e.g. sitting in a traffic jam when you are late. This can also be helpful in controlling unpleasant panic attacks. This exercise is called 'W.A.S.P.' for short:

Wait: Say '**stop**' to yourself.
Absorb: Take a deep breath, breathe out slowly and pull shoulders down, absorb the situation. Tell yourself to relax and stop fussing.
Slowly: When you feel calm, slowly....
Proceed: Carry on with what you were doing but in a more relaxed frame of mind.

Eating, drinking and living wisely

Regular eating is important when you are experiencing a busy, stressful lifestyle. Little and often is the key here, then the stomach does not become overloaded. Breakfast is probably the most important meal so don't miss it! It will give you increased energy throughout the day, especially if you eat wholegrain (unrefined) cereals, yogurt and fresh fruit. If you are already under stress, watch your diet! You may be eating and drinking things which can increase your stress levels. Here are some DOs and DON'Ts.

DO'S
1. Do eat protein: fish, lean meat, cheese, yogurt, skimmed milk.
2. Do eat vitamin B: whole-grain breads, cereals, yeast extracts.
3. Do eat vitamin C: citrus fruits, peppers, baked potatoes, strawberries.
4. Do eat vitamin A: dark green and yellow vegetables, pulses.

DON'T'S
1. Limit caffeine: coffee, tea, chocolate, cocoa and headache pills.
2. Limit refined products: sugar, white flour and processed foods - if possible cut them out completely.
3. Don't add salt to your food: most foods already contain enough salt.
4. Limit foods which are high in saturated fat: fried and convenience foods, hamburgers, sausages and chips.
5. Don't drink too much alcohol, although moderate drinking appears to do no harm.
6. Don't eat when tense. In fact it is a good idea to practise a minute or two of relaxation before you eat any meal.
7. And above all don't smoke! You may think this gives you a short-term relaxing effect, but in fact nicotine makes the problem worse.

Posture.

Poor posture can also contribute to stress. If you are busy all day, do check that your body is well balanced and that your muscles are relaxed without causing you to slouch. No crossed knees, ankles or arms please! Bad posture wastes energy and prevents the body from functioning properly. Watch the position of your head. It is very heavy so if it is out of balance it increases postural stress.

Exercise.

Do you get enough exercise? Exercise is very necessary if you lead a busy pressurised life. You must exercise to ensure a strong heart and circulation and it is a good way of relieving tension.

Swimming, walking and cycling are probably the best, but any exercise is good. Gym and exercise classes are very popular now so you have no excuse! Movements combine with relaxation - it is great for taking your mind off your problems too.

Remember also to have regular medical checks.

Sleep.

To encourage sleep, a slow winding-down process before bed is helpful. Try some of the following - different things suit different people. A warm bath or a glass of warm milk and honey or a short walk may be helpful. Move slowly, watch funny, light-hearted or soothing television programmes, do not argue, keep lights and music low and relax before bed.

Try not to take drugs unless the problem has got out of hand and then only take them for a short time to restore a sleep pattern. Above all learn a technique to help you to switch your mind off. You may find the relaxation or breathing exercises described earlier will help you to sleep.

Relationships and communications

At home

Stress at home can be caused by misunderstanding and poor communications. Parents often take too much on their own shoulders and children do not always live up to idealist expectations. Families are made up of groups of individuals with differing needs and goals in life. Listening and communicating are essential elements of a relaxed home life.

It is particularly important to allow yourself time to relax after work before launching into domestic problems.

At work

Stress at work is often caused by misunderstandings and personality clashes.

Learn how to take these in your stride and be confident in your own abilities and limitations - don't be forced into taking on tasks which are beyond your ability and don't be afraid to say 'no'.

It is best to be assertive in your relationships with work colleagues - don't just give in, yet at the same time don't feel you always have to be aggressive to achieve your goals.

Reducing stress in relationships

Learn to be confident in relationships at work and at home. Mark the points which are particularly relevant to you. Try and practise them each day:

- Be aware of your own feelings - anger, sadness, rejection etc - and tell others.
- Don't explode or sulk and hide away.
- Use 'I' statements, e.g. 'I think it would be better if' rather than blaming 'you' statements, e.g. 'You messed that up...'
- Be aware of what others want to communicate - become a good listener and let others have their say.
- Don't ever assume things about others.
- Give people your time and respect.
- Co-operate. Be a member of a team both at home and at work.
- Ask for help and support when needed.
- Allow yourself to love and be loved.
- Talk to someone you trust.
- Accept what you cannot change.
- If you are sick, don't try and pretend you're not.
- Be realistic about perfection and what you can achieve.
- 'Switch off' after work - before you walk into the house.
- Allow yourself ten minutes rest period when you get home before exploding about your day.
- Learn to like yourself.
- Emphasise your good points.
- Agree with someone for a change.
- Don't take yourself too seriously.
- Have an equal balance between working, home and social life.
- Don't be afraid to say 'no'.
- Use relaxed body language, smile and laugh.
- Defend your rights and personal space without abusing or dominating others.
- Be committed to what you are doing in every area of your life.

Now make a note of any points which you feel will help YOU to reduce your stress levels and be a more confident communicator. Write them into your personal space so that you can practise them; ask someone else who knows you well to help you achieve these.

personal space

Using time wisely

A busy person is not necessarily under stress, and getting rid of stress does not mean being slow. You must have time to feel a sense of accomplishment. It is up to you how you use the twenty-four hours in a day!

It is important to plan your day as well as planning the month and year. You must spend time to make time and make sure this includes leisure time, exercise and holidays. If you manage your time well it will reduce stress.

Everybody has a 'Prime Time' - morning or evening. Sort out when your own personal 'Prime Time' is. Important tasks which demand time, energy and concentration should be done when you are feeling fresh and energetic. Try hard not to let yourself be disturbed during this time.

When is YOUR 'Prime Time'? Mark your 'Prime Time' in your personal space, so you can aim to do the most important things during this time each day, and ask people not to disturb you at this time.

Ask yourself these three key questions:
- Are you completely satisfied with the way you use your time?
- If not, why not?
- What could you have done to use your time more satisfactorily?

Prime Time: personal space

Reduce stress by managing your time

- Learn to say NO. Effectiveness depends upon knowing what not to do.
- Overcommitment is a sure road to failure!
- Decide what you want to get out of the day.
- Make a list of things you HAVE to do and the things you would like to do, with time estimates.
- Decide what only YOU must do. These are your priorities. Delegate the rest.
- Select an order or sequence for tasks to be done - important jobs first.
- Try to do one task at a time otherwise you get muddled.
- Don't rush immediately from one task to another. Instead PAUSE, RELAX and use breaks wisely.
- Don't set yourself too high standards - be realistic about what you can achieve.
- At the end of the day, remember what you HAVE achieved and give yourself credit for it.
- At the end of the day, tidy up ready for tomorrow.
- Don't answer the telephone when you don't wish to be disturbed.
- Intersperse dull jobs with interesting ones, tiring jobs with easier ones.
- Don't waste time feeling GUILTY about what you could not do. Discipline yourself to work during work time, and allow yourself time to relax each day when you can completely switch off.
- DO take holidays! Take a few regular short breaks or days off if you can't take a long holiday.
- Find yourself an absorbing hobby that is completely removed from routine work - go out of your way to create a diversion for yourself.

Now make a note in your personal space of any points which you feel will help YOU to reduce your stress levels and plan your time better. Then draw up a plan for next week, including your 'Prime Time' and plan ahead WHAT you intend to do and WHEN. Review what you have done and reward yourself for any improvements you have made (you will have also lowered your stress level!)

personal space

Controlling your stress

Here is a summary action plan to control your stress, depending which section of the stress/burnout scale you felt you were on.(page 14) Try to bring yourself closer to the optimum level of stress, and seek a stress counsellor or go to your doctor if you feel you may be approaching 'burnout'.

Do you remember where you were on the stress/burnout scale on page 14?

Too little stress	Optimum stress	Too much stress	Burnout
DO	**DO**	**DO**	**DO**
Take up a hobby	Maintain this level	Realise you are important	Seek professional help if you have reached this area
Meet people every day	Relax every day	Relax every day	Arrange regular sessions with a counsellor or stress consultant until you can help yourself
Chat to people	Keep things in perspective	Take gentle exercise	
Think positively	Exercise	Do things more slowly	
Exercise or walk	Healthy diet	Confide in a friend, or talk to a counsellor	
Have a cat or dog	Know when to stop	Take one thing at a time	
Do some work every day	Take adequate rest and sleep	Give yourself time and space	
Eat a balanced diet	Maintain good relationships		
Listen to music	Be comfortable		
Read a newspaper	Organise priorities		
Read a book			

How much progress have you made?

Can you now say "yes" to each of the following? If so, well done!! Read through the statements and complete your own personal action plan on the next page.

Can you say No?

Are you organised?

Can you prioritise?

Are you able to delegate?

Can you seek help when necessary?

Can you manage your time well?

Are you able to be definite in your thinking and hence avoid uncertainties?

Are you doing the most suitable job?

Are you aware of what stress is all about and what causes stress?

Can you recognise the signs and symptoms of stress?

Are you able to talk to people freely about your feelings?

Are you in a good state of health?

Do you feel secure and value yourself?

Do you enjoy a healthy balanced diet?

Do you have a low caffeine and alcohol consumption?

Have you stopped or reduced smoking habits?

Do you exercise regularly?

Do you smile and laugh?

Are you a positive thinker?

Are you learning to be more confident when dealing with people?

Your personal action plan

First remind yourself of your key stressors - that is the things around you or changes which you said make you stressed. Then write down your action plan - what you are going to do to control your stress.

Your stressors.
What are your main stressors? Look back at pages 8 to 13.

Breathing.
Which breathing exercise will you try from pages 16 and 17?

YOUR ACTION	WHEN

Relaxation.
Which relaxation exercises will you try from pages 18 and 19?

YOUR ACTION	WHEN

Eating and Drinking.
How will you change your eating and drinking habits?

YOUR ACTION	WHEN

Lifestyle.
How will you change your posture? What exercise will you take up? How will you improve your sleeping patterns? (if you need to)

YOUR ACTION	WHEN

Communication.
Which of the points from page 23 will you put into action?

YOUR ACTION	WHEN

Time management.
Which of the points from pages 24 and 25 will you put into action?

YOUR ACTION	WHEN

and last but not least.... have fun!

Stressdots: How to use them

Now you understand better what makes you stressed and how to reduce your stress. You are ready to use your Stressdots - on the front of this guide. They are your own personal stress monitor and they can be worn throughout the day.

At the foot of the Stressdot card you will find a strip of ten black dots.

How they work

The Stressdots work on the temperature of your hands.

When you are under stress there is an increase in muscle tension, the blood vessels near the skin's surface constrict and the temperature of your hands and feet decreases. Similarly, as you relax, your hands and feet become warmer and blood flows more freely. Watch your dot change colour as you work and relax.

Your Stressdot will also be affected by room temperature - a warm room or sunshine will warm your hands and change the colour of the Stressdots.

You are likely to be more relaxed when in a warmer room. However, if strong sunshine affects the colour of your Stressdots, cover the dot with the thumb of your other hand for a few seconds, then check the colour.

The history of Stressdots

Stressdots have been developed and tested over many years by stress professionals in response to requests from patients for a portable and inexpensive stress monitor which they could take home with them and use on a daily basis.

They have been widely used for over 10 years by individuals and stress counsellors to provide fast and accurate feedback and to help individuals understand and control their own stress levels - particularly in the case of potential sufferers of heart disease.

We hope you will find them both helpful and fun to use - an anxious lady, for instance, was given a Stressdot to wear while doing her relaxation exercises, to see how she was getting on. It was brown when she started and blue when she had finished relaxing both physically and mentally. It remained blue as she chatted for the next half hour, but as soon as the doorbell rang and she saw a salesman outside it immediately turned back to brown! Try out your Stressdots now and find out how YOUR body responds in different situations.